fantastic ideas for
maths outdoors

KIRSTINE BEELEY

Published 2013 by Featherstone Education
Bloomsbury Publishing plc
50 Bedford Square, London, WC1B 3DP
www.bloomsbury.com

Bloomsbury is a registered trademark of Bloomsbury Publishing Plc

ISBN 978-1-4081-8679-4

Text © Kirstine Beeley 2013
Design © Lynda Murray
Photographs © Shutterstock, Kirstine Beeley

Printed and bound in India by Replika Press Pvt. Ltd.

This book is produced using paper that is made from wood grown in
managed, sustainable forests. It is natural, renewable and recyclable.
The logging and manufacturing processes conform to the environmental
regulations of the country of origin.

5 6 7 8 9 10

To see our full range of titles visit **www.bloomsbury.com**

Acknowledgements
Thanks to the staff and children of Treehouse Preschool, Winslow, Bucks for their
time and patience in helping put this book together, including the use of a number
of photographs.
Photographs p48 and p59 reproduced with kind permission of London Early Years
Foundation/Emli Bendixen.

Contents

Introduction

The key to providing good outdoor learning experiences is to view your outdoor environment as a unique opportunity to develop skills, language and understanding and not just as a carbon copy of your indoor provision. Outdoor learning is not about bringing the indoors outdoors but about embracing all that the outdoors has to offer and using that to provide fun, inspiring and engaging opportunities for children to learn through play.

Although this book looks at ideas for exploring maths outdoors, it is important to acknowledge that many of the activities are designed not just to develop mathematical thinking but also to aid development in other areas. A counting activity may help to develop talking skills or a sorting activity might aid fine motor control. In children's early years of learning rarely does an experience offer only one learning opportunity.

When thinking about developing your outdoor provision you should look at your existing offering and ask yourself 'what makes this outdoor learning?' Is the equipment different from what you provide indoors or are you using the same small plastic buckets and spades in the outdoor sand as you are indoors? Outdoors offers unique access to space allowing the exploration of larger equipment, noisier and more physical activities, great for those learners who need to be moving about (kinaesthetic learners) or those who find the noise levels indoors too distracting (even though it can be noisier outdoors, the lack of walls and ceilings makes listening and hence talking much easier).

Outdoor learning must also hold equal importance in your planning to indoor learning and just as much thought needs to go into what resources you provide to stimulate children's curiosity, enthusiasm and thirst for learning. There are lots of elaborate and often expensive resources available to enhance your outdoor learning, many of which are well beyond the budgets of most early years settings. With this in mind, the activities in this book have been developed with limited budgets in mind and include resources which are freely available at home or even free.

When planning to enhance your maths provision remember it's not all about knowing your numbers, there is lots of sorting, matching, counting, patterning and measuring for children to do if they are to gain a good understanding of what number actually is and not just be able to reel off numbers in order by rote. Always make sure you include zero in your counting activities and give children lots of opportunities to explore and understand an empty set. Outdoor learning provides a myriad of maths learning opportunities, only a selection of which are included in this book. Wherever possible use these ideas as your starting point and follow the children's lead in taking the learning forward. Enjoy the outdoors for all that it offers and make sure it's available to access in all weathers... learning shouldn't stop just because its cold or raining!

Skin allergy alert

Some detergents and soaps can cause skin reactions.
Always be mindful of potential skin allergies when letting children mix anything with their hands and always provide lots of facilities to wash materials off after they have been in contact with the skin. Watch out for this symbol on the relevant pages.

Food allergy alert

When using food stuffs to enhance your play opportunties always be mindful of potential food allergies. We have used this symbol on the relevant pages.

Bucket maths

What you need:

- **A wide selection of aluminium buckets** (available from garden centres, Swedish furniture stores in the flower section and florist sections in craft shops)
- **Water**
- **Sand**
- **Numbers** (1-10)
- **Flower pots**
- **Compost/soil**

Taking it forward

- Try filling the buckets with sand and making a line of sandcastles from small to large.
- Stick plastic numbers on the front of the buckets and put them in numer order.
- Hang the buckets on a vertical string or wire with the smallest at the top. Pour water in from the top and watch it cascade down as you continue pouring.
- Use different sized terracotta flowerpots in your planting area and encourage children to explore the different sizes as they fill them with compost and soil.

What's in it for the children?

This is a great activity for helping children to really appreciate the concept of size and ordering. It allows children to physically explore size as part of other outdoor activities with sand, mud or water.

What to do:

1. Encourage the children to explore the different sizes and capacities of the buckets in a wide variety of outdoor situations.

2. Try ordering the buckets in a line from smallest to biggest.

3. Nest them inside each other. How many can you fit inside one another?

4. Can you build a tower with the biggest bucket at the bottom?

5. Fill with water and explore which holds the most, least etc. How many little buckets fill a bigger one?

Balloon hoopla

- Balloons
- Helium canister (available from party stores or large supermarkets)
- String or gift wrap ribbon
- Large stones or pebbles
- Hula hoops
- Marker pens
- Dice

What to do:

1. Inflate the balloons with the helium and draw large numbers on them.

2. Tether the balloons to the pebbles, each using a different length of string so that the balloons are hovering at different heights weighted down by the pebbles.

3. Encourage children to pick up the hula-hoops and toss them over a particular number.

Top tip ★

If you use balloons specifically for helium they will stay inflated longer.

Taking it forward

- Try rolling a large dice and then hoopla a balloon that matches the number on the dice.

- Try rolling two dice and hoopla the answer.

- Can you get the hoop over a number one more or one less?

- Draw shapes on the balloon and encourage the children to hoopla specific shapes or colours.

What's in it for the children?

This is a really physical way of playing with numbers. It requires lots of gross motor skills and builds on hand eye co-ordination as children explore all sorts of numbers, shapes and colours in a fun and interactive way. Great for encouraging children to turn take too!

Going potty!

What you need:

- A variety of different sized flower pots
- Blackboard paint
- Chalks
- A selection of natural materials for counting including pine cones, pebbles, shells, conkers, sticks, gravel, seeds etc.

What to do:

1. Paint the outside of the pots with blackboard paint (available from most hardware stores).

2. Use the chalks to write numbers on the outside of the pots.

3. Encourage children to place the pots in order either counting forwards or backwards.

4. Now have fun putting the correct number of objects into each of the pots.

5. Using different sized pots encourages problem solving skills as children select different sized materials to fit in the pots. 4 pinecones may not fit in 1 pot but 4 acorns might.

Taking it forward

- Using small terracotta pots (available in florist sections of craft stores), encourage children to count and order the pots on a much smaller scale. Try using small loose parts such as seeds, petals or gravel to count into the pots.

- Use large sturdy pots, turn upside down and make a pot stepping stone number line (make sure the pots are sturdy enough to hold the children's weight and that they don't topple over when stood on).

- Under adult supervision try to build a plant pot tower (using plastic plant pots with numbers on is a child friendly way of adapting this activity) with the biggest number at the bottom.

- Draw the same number e.g. 5 on to lots of diffrent pots and let children count the right number of objects into each pot.

Health & Safety

Always check pots before use as water and frost can cause cracks and faults in pots when left outdoors.

What's in it for the children?

This is a really nice outdoor slant on making number lines. Children are able to recognise and talk about numbers, order them and then count into sets. If children are encouraged to write their own numbers they are developing more skills. With different sized pots there are lots of opportunity to develop size language (big, bigger, biggest etc.) as well as size sorting and problem solving.

There's a hole in my brick!

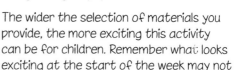

What you need:

- Air bricks from a builder's merchant or friendly builder
- A wide selection of natural materials including sticks, leaves, flowers, seeds etc. (anything that children can poke into the holes in the bricks)

What to do:

1. Allow the children to freely explore the bricks with the objects provided.

2. Encourage the children to sort the objects according to their own criteria. They may chose to see if they can find sticks that fit in the holes or order twigs from shortest to longest. They may sort flowers or leaves according to shape or size.

Top tip ⭐

The wider the selection of materials you provide, the more exciting this activity can be for children. Remember what looks exciting at the start of the week may not look quite so exciting by mid week!

Taking it forward

- Why not have a go at upsizing this activity by providing upturned bread crates or milk crates and big pieces of bark, large branches or sticks and pine cones or fruit (apples etc.)

- Make a pattern in the top row of a brick (i.e. short twig, long twig or blue flower, yellow flower) and see if the children can copy the pattern on the next row of holes down.

What's in it for the children?

This activity allows children to sort and match objects according to their own simple criteria and if they choose to they can explore simple patterns and develop their mathematical language surrounding size.

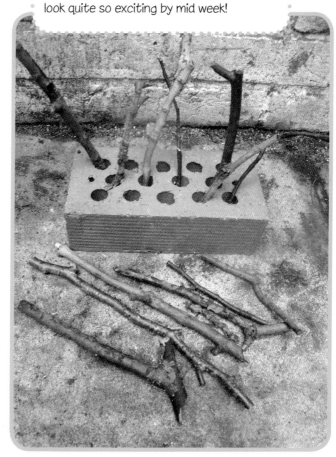

Clay number exploration

What you need:

- **Some sticky clay** (either from ground if in a clay soil area – clean of course) **or air-drying clay from a craft or education supplier**
- **Laminated number cards**
- **A wide selection of natural materials including twigs, acorns, seeds, conkers, shells, stones, pebbles, etc.**
- **Coloured glass beads**
- **Flat surface for rolling clay**
- **Water** (to keep clay moist and malleable)

Taking it forward

- Make clay numerals that have the corresponding number of objects attached i.e. number 2 decorated with 2 acorns, 2 glass beads, 2 feathers etc.

- Make large-scale clay numbers and decorate as a group (discussing how many of each object you need to place on each number) and use to decorate a wall or fence (a lovely sensory number line).

What's in it for the children?

As part of ongoing exploration of numbers and numerals, children are able to explore the characteristics of the clay and enjoy exploring other natural materials. This is a good way of combining expressive art and design with maths.

What to do:

1. Make lots of long 'snakes' with the clay. Lay the appropriate number of snakes over the chosen number card and squash down so you have a flatter clay numeral (not too flat or it will break when it hardens).

2. Encourage children to decorate their numbers with the natural materials.

3. Make a hole through the top edge of the number with a pencil and leave to dry out.

4. When hardened, you can either just thread the numbers and hang from a fence or a number tree or use varnish to preserve before using to decorate your outdoor area.

Top tip ⭐

Add a fair bit of water to the clay before exploring it - it will last longer before it dries out and will allow children to decorate it more easily.

Big bucket fun

What you need:

- **A selection of plastic buckets in a variety of large sizes** (try your local scrap store – see useful addresses). **Use car wash buckets and DIY and building buckets. Clear buckets are ideal so children can see the water levels through the sides**

- Water

- Food colouring

What to do:

1. Fill a selection of the smaller buckets with different coloured water using food colouring.

2. Allow children to explore transferring the water into the bigger buckets. Talk about how far up the big bucket the water is going. Can you mark it with a pen? What will happen if you add another bucket of water?

3. Encourage children to explore filling the smaller buckets from the bigger buckets. Talk about full, empty, big, bigger, and biggest.

4. How many small buckets do the children think it will take to fill a big bucket? How many smaller buckets will one big bucket fill?

Taking it forward

- Use a wider selection of clear containers such as food pots, plastic milk bottles etc. to encourage more discussion about the measuring of water from one container to another.

- Try building a water obstacle course. Children have to carry small containers of coloured water across obstacles to the end where they pour the water into the big container until it reaches a mark where the game ends.

What's in it for the children?

Children find the concept of big, bigger and biggest a lot easier to understand if they use really big objects. Outdoors offers the chance to work on a scale not really available indoors, especially not with water play. Working with water allows children to explore the language of capacity (full, fuller, empty etc.) as well as being great from prediction and early measuring skills.

Top tip ⭐

Don't forget to talk about what happens when the colours mix.

Counting sand casts

What you need:

- Sand
- Card strips
- Paper clips
- A selection of natural materials including pebbles, shells, twigs, etc. (NOT conkers or acorns as they will go mouldy when left outside)
- Plaster of Paris
- Water
- A throw away cup or container
- A stick for mixing

Taking it forward

- Add extra sand counters with plastic numbers set in them so children can match them in the sand.
- Draw different numbers on the ground with chalk and see if the children can match the sand number discs to these.

What's in it for the children?

This is a lovely fun creative activity which makes a really open-ended natural and very sensory resource that children can use and adapt to many, many counting and sorting outdoor activities.

Top tip ⭐

NEVER pour unused plaster down a drain or sink. Always dispose of it in a bin.

What to do:

1. Paper clip your card strip to make a circle and push slightly into the surface of the sand.
2. Press a number of the same natural objects into the sand inside the circle i.e. 2 shells, 4 pebbles etc.
3. Mix the plaster of Paris according to the instructions using a stick.
4. Pour the plaster into the card mould on top of your objects.
5. Be careful at this point – as the plaster reacts and hardens it gets really hot. Wait until it has cooled a bit to let children feel the heat.
6. When it is hard (a few hours later or overnight is ideal), remove the card ring and take out your sand counter. Brush away any excess sand to reveal your counting objects.
7. Use the disks in the sand to encourage children to count and place in order.

Colour hunt matching

What you need:

- A set of colour paint charts (free from DIY stores)
- A shaped hole punch
- A binder ring or treasury tag
- A selection of different coloured tiles or cards

Taking it forward

- Stick strips of double sided tape onto some card in rows and stick a coloured sticker at one end. When children have found something which matches their colour sticker they can stick it on the tape with the appropriate colour row.

- Put out a selection of natural materials (leaves, petals, wood, pebbles etc.). Ask children to sort into baskets with colours pegged onto them.

- Put a selection of coloured tiles or cards out on the grass or chalk coloured circles onto pavements and see if children can find things to match and sort into the correct places.

What's in it for the children?

Children need lots of opportunities to sort, match and count using different materials. The natural world provides beautiful objects to explore, sort and match with. The colour cards help children to match according to colour and build an awareness of the existence of different shades of a particular colour.

What to do:

1. Punch out a shape (like the tree in the photo) at the end of each of the colours on the card with the hole punch.

2. Repeat for other colour chart cards.

3. See if you can match the cards to objects in your outdoor area. Laying the card on top of the object will allow you to see the colour of the object through the shape hole.

4. Can you make a collection of things which are a certain colour? i.e. lots of different shades of green things.

> ### Top tip ⭐
>
> Use a binder ring or a treasury tag to keep your colour cards together and give you something to hang them up by.

pavement painting

What you need:

- A selection of different coloured pavement chalks
- Some zip lock food bags
- A mallet or hammer
- Pots
- Water
- Paintbrushes

What to do:

1. Place a piece of coloured chalk into your zip lock bag.

2. Now crush the chalk to a fine powder using a hammer.

3. Place some of the powder into a shallow pot and mix with a little water until you get a paint-like consistency.

4. Now you can either paint numbers onto the pavement and wait for them to dry and then encourage children to paint back over them with water and paint brushes, or you can draw numbers on the ground with the chalk and get children to explore painting their own numbers over the top with their chalk paints.

Taking it forward

- Put sets of natural objects such as pinecones etc. into circles drawn on the floor. Ask children to write or chalk paint the correct number on the ground next to that number of objects. Alternatively, paint the correct numbers randomly nearby and ask children to run a skipping rope from the set to the numeral. (This is set matching on a very large scale).

- Paint shapes onto the ground with chalk paint then ask children to look for objects outdoors that are that shape and place them on the set.

What's in it for the children?

A great way of exploring materials, playing with numbers on a large scale and encouraging children to explore and engage with the outdoor learning environment.

Top tip ⭐

if you don't have pavement chalk use a mixture of cornflour, water and paint or food colouring - it works just as well as pavement paint.

Ice jewel patterns

What you need:

- Water
- Food colouring
- Ice cube trays in a variety of shapes
- Access to a freezer (or outdoors overnight in winter)
- Snowy or really frosty weather!

What to do:

1. Mix up the water in a wide variety of bright colours.
2. Pour into the ice cube trays and freeze or leave out over night if you know the temperature will drop low enough to freeze the water.
3. Empty the ice cubes into a bowl.
4. Encourage children to use the ice shapes to make coloured patterns of ice jewels on the frosty or snowy ground. Encourage lots of patterning using both colours and shapes. Can children make their own shapes? Can they carry on a pattern you have started?

Taking it forward

- Try freezing coloured water in balloons and making large-scale coloured patterns with the resulting coloured ice balls.
- In summer use ice jewels to make patterns in sand instead of snow.

What's in it for the children?

Children need lots of chances to explore pattern in a wide variety of situations. This activity lets them explore making and continuing patterns according to shape and colour whilst interacting with their surrounding and the weather first hand. A great combination of early maths and early science exploration.

Stick patterns

- Clay
- Thin straight twigs or wooden kebab skewers
- A collection of different coloured leaves and petals

What to do:

1. Stick a twig or skewer into a ball of clay or into soft ground so it sticks up vertically.

2. Select leaves or petals and stick them onto the twigs to make a recurring pattern e.g. green, brown, green, brown or large, small, large, small etc. Encourage the children to carry on with the pattern.

Taking it forward

- Once children are able to carry on an existing pattern, encourage them to make their own patterns. Do they make patterns according to colour, size, shape etc.?

- Try laying leaves in a line on the ground to make a pattern and see if you can carry it on?

- Can they use the leaves and petals to make a design on the ground or on a log slice?

What's in it for the children?

Children need lots of opportunities to explore patterning with a wide variety of materials. Using leaves and petals offers an opportunity to work with and explore patterns and other mathematical concepts such as size, shape etc. with materials unique to the outdoor environment.

Leaf play

What you need:

- A wide selection of leaves of different shapes, colours and sizes
- A hole punch
- String or wool
- Large plastic sewing needles

What to do:

1. Using the hole punch make holes through the leaves.

2. Encourage children to choose a big leaf first. Thread the leaf onto the thread or string.

3. Now ask children to find a smaller leaf and thread that. Keep going until they have a string of decreasing sized leaves.

4. When finished you can hang these from trees, a branch or a fence to display and to encourage further discussion. Try again starting with an even bigger or a very small leaf.

Taking it forward

- Place a thin stick (or wooden barbecue skewer) into a lump of clay or play dough so that it stands vertically. Push leaves onto your stick starting with the biggest first (or smallest).

What's in it for the children?

This activity allows children to really explore the concept of size and to get to grips with mathematical language about size. Using big, bigger, biggest, small, smaller, smallest etc. at the same time as they are exploring natural materials, develops early fine motor skills (essential for pre-writing).

Top tip ⭐

Use a single hole punch to get a good threading hole.

Log books

What you need:

- **A selection of log slices** (available from tree surgeons or your local council parks management dept)
- **Blackboard paint**
- **Chalk in a variety of colours**

What to do:

1. Paint the log slices with a number of coats of paint until you have a good smooth coating to the centre of the log.

2. Encourage children to write and mark make on the logs using the chalks. A duster mitt or a woolen glove is great for wiping off after use.

Taking it forward

- Try building 'log books' in a variety of sizes. A huge one will encourage children to mark make together.

- Try painting the top of a big tree stump log for a write on table top or paint some logs with yacht varnish and use dry wipe markers instead.

What's in it for the children?

Children need lots of exciting and inviting opportunities to write and mark make. This activity offers a chance to do that in a uniquely outdoors way, ensuring that it's not just the activity which is outdoors but the materials too.

Top tip ⭐

A coat of wood preservative prior to painting will help to stop the wood splitting as it dries.

Step on it

What you need:

- Vinyl material
- A selection of log slices (available from your local woodland trust or council groundsman or tree surgeon)
- Acrylic paint
- Pavement chalks
- Dice

What to do:

1. Use the vinyl material (cut into number shapes) and stick on the log slice with hard wearing glue or use acrylic paint or chalk to paint on the numbers.

2. Encourage the children to place slices in order, asking questions such as 'which number comes next?' 'How many is one more?' etc. as you work together to build the number line.

3. Once the number line is complete, encourage the children to explore it by stepping across the numbers counting as they go. Encourage children to count both forwards and backwards.

Top tip ★

Always remember to include zero in your number line. Don't make your log slices too big and heavy as children need to be able to lift them and move them around safely.

Taking it forward

- Ask the children to move forwards or backwards a certain number of places 'can you move forwards two?' 'Move backwards 3, etc.

- Ask children to show you one more or one less by moving up and down the number line.

- Ask the children to stand on a number, roll a big dice and get them to move that number forwards or backwards.

- Take out a number from the number line (or turn it over so you can't see it) and see if children can work out which number is missing.

- Mix the numbers up and see how quickly children can put them back in order.

- Sing number line songs like 'Five little men in a flying saucer' or 'Five little ducks' and ask children to move down the number line as they sing. Why not be the frogs in 'Five little speckled frogs' and jump off your log while singing the song.

- Let children write their own numbers on the log slices to be able to make their own number lines. How far can they make them go?

What's in it for the children?

As well as being able to recognise numerals, children also need to be able to order the numbers as this is a basic skill used later in life for addition and subtraction. Using stepping stones makes this a very physical experience of number, ideal for your kinesthetic learners.

Shaping up nicely

- A large sheet of white paper
- Marker pen
- A large sheet of clear sticky back plastic
- A wide selection of natural materials including leaves, twigs, petals, acorns, conkers, etc.

What to do:

1. On the white sheet of paper draw a selection of shapes including shapes of different sizes.

2. Carefully take the backing paper off the sticky back paper and place it sticky side upwards on top of the shape paper.

3. Encourage children to use the natural materials to copy over the top of the shapes and to make their own shapes. Encourage them to talk about size as well as shape as they will need small things to make smaller shapes.

4. At the end of the activity it is possible to stick the sheet to a window to preserve your nature shapes and to provide a great window display.

Taking it forward

- Make up smaller versions of the activity on smaller pieces of card for individuals to complete themselves or in pairs. These can be turned over and stuck to card and displayed by hanging from fences or trees outside afterwards.

What's in it for the children?

Children need lots of opportunities to see and explore shapes in lots of different situations. This activity allows then to explore shape at the same time as working with lots if natural materials. It encourages individual creativity as well as providing an ideal opportunity to develop early fine motor skills.

Top tip ★

Place the sticky back plastic flat on top of the sheet of paper and peel the paper off as horizontally as you can to avoid creasing.

Nice ice numbers

What you need:

- Warm water
- Paint or coloured chalk
- DIY paint brushes
- Cold weather
- **Squirty bottles** (the type used in gardening or hairdressing) **available from pound shops**

Taking it forward

- Have a go at painting a number line onto a frosty surface.
- Squirt coloured warm water onto snow to form rainbow numbers.
- The afternoon before a frosty or snowy night try forming numbers with salt on different surfaces and see if the numbers show up in the morning where the frost or snow has not been able to freeze.
- Try squirting coloured patterns onto snow with your warm coloured paint.

What's in it for the children?

Whilst exploring ways of forming numerals (physical development) children are able to see melting numerals as well. This is very much an activity focused on number recognition rather than counting.

Top tip ⭐

If you know an overnight frost is forecast, chalk some numbers onto a surface so that children can trace over them through the frost with their warm water brushes.

What to do:

1. On a cold and frosty (or snowy) morning don't avoid going outdoors, embrace the cold as a chance to explore numbers and numerals in a unique way with a sensory experience not available at any other time of the year.

2. Provide children with pots of warm watered down coloured paint (or water with coloured chalk mixed in).

3. Encourage children to paint with warm water onto frosty surfaces to form melted numbers. Then encourage children to find objects to put with their numerals.

✚ Health & Safety
Always be mindful of creating slippery surfaces when adding water to cold, frosty or snowy areas.

Mud brick patterning

What you need:

- Mud
- Water
- Ice cube trays
- Paint or powder paint

What to do:

1. Mix some mud with water until you have a sticky consistency but not too runny.

2. Mould your mud into the ice cube trays, making sure to pack it down as hard as possible.

3. Leave either in the sun or somewhere warm to dry out.

4. Turn out your mini mud bricks.

5. Repeat the process adding a little powder paint to the mud to create coloured mud bricks.

6. When you have a selection of mud bricks encourage the children to build with them making patterns according to shapes and colours. Can they make a line of blue brick, brown brick, blue brick etc. or given a line of bricks in a pattern (say red, brown, red, brown) can the children build a matching line of bricks on top?

Taking it forward

- Make the bricks available for children to use as part of their ongoing play.
- Paint real bricks with paint and make big brick patterns.
- Colour in patterns on bricks on walls in the outdoors area.
- Talk about rectangles. Can you find any around the setting or on the way to or from the setting?

What's in it for the children?

This is a great way for children to explore simple patterns with a uniquely outdoors resource. As well as exploring colour and shape patterns, it helps children to begin to look for shapes in their surroundings and to be able to recognise patterns in everyday objects such as walls and paths. With the small bricks, children will be developing their fine motor and co-ordination skills as they build.

Top tip ⭐

Don't make your mud too sloppy or it won't dry out and won't stay together when dry.

Match it Up

What you need:

- A wide selection of natural materials including acorns, conkers, leaves, pine cones etc. (You will need two of each object – try to make sure they are of a similar size and shape)

- A small cloth bag, an old sock or old tissue or baby wipe box with a hole for your hand

What to do:

1. Place the objects in your container.

2. Ask a child to reach in and take out an object, encouraging them to take time to feel and talk about the texture, size shape etc. of the object before they pull it out.

3. Now encourage the child to place their hand in the container and try and find the matching natural object. Can they find another 'spiky one' or 'another smooth acorn'? Encourage lots of language to describe the texture as well as the size and shape of the objects.

Taking it forward

- Use off-cuts of wood and glue natural objects onto each end to create nature dominoes. Can the children arrange them by matching say two acorns or two red leaves?

- Place a natural object in the bottom of a clear two litre plastic bottle with the top cut off to form a cylinder container. Add other objects to other cylinders. Place a pile of natural objects near to the cylinders. Encourage children to sort the objects into the cylinders. Can they count them at the end or as they go? Which has the most objects? When children get confident at this try using a timer to see how quickly they can do the 'Nature sorting challenge'.

- Try different collections to sort such as a big pile of different coloured leaves, a selection of small objects or shells etc.

What's in it for the children?

Simple sorting and matching skills are key to early mathematical thinking. Children can explore concepts of colour, shape and size as they play with these unique natural materials.

Nature number lines

What you need:

- A selection of natural materials including acorns, pinecones, twigs, leaves, conkers etc.
- Pieces of string (different lengths)
- A long stick (about 1 metre long)

What to do:

1. Thread different numbers of natural objects onto strings. Make the strings differing lengths dependent upon the numbers of objects (short string for 1, longer for 5 etc.).

2. Tie the strings in numerical order onto the stick and hang in your outdoor area where children are able to touch as well as see and count the objects.

Taking it forward

- Give children number cards and ask them to peg or stick them to the strings with the corresponding number of objects.

- Place number cards on the floor and place numbers of objects next to the cards.

- Thread acorns onto string and knot both ends so that you have a series of acorn strings with differing numbers of acorns. Encourage children to order the acorn strings and/or match them to number cards or acorns with numbers written on them.

What's in it for the children?

Children need to be able to count sets of objects in many, many different situations. Nature number lines allow children to see very visually how numbers increase in quantity.

Top tip ⭐

The more variety of number lines you use the more children will have a chance to count.

Nature patterns

- Large sheet clear sticky back plastic
- A wide selection of natural materials including shells, pinecones, conkers, acorns, leaves, twigs etc.
- String
- Threading needles
- Sellotape

Taking it forward

- Why not develop your string patterns and hang them up in sets from a bigger stick to form a nature pattern mobile which can be hung from a fence or tree.

- When patterns have been made on the sticky plastic it can be stuck to a window to give a great nature effect decoration that children can keep referring to or adding to if you stick the plastic sticky side facing outwards.

What's in it for the children?

As well as developing hand eye coordination, children are able to explore lots of patterning with uniquely outdoor materials and discuss and build on their understanding of size, colour and shape.

What to do:

Method 1

1. Peel back the paper from the sticky back plastic and lay it sticky side up on the floor or on a flat surface.

2. Use the natural materials to form the start of a pattern on the sticky paper i.e. a leaf then a shell, leaf, shell etc. or red leaf, yellow leaf etc.

3. Encourage children to carry on the pattern themselves and then to create their own patterns.

Method 2

1. Drill holes through conkers, acorns etc. (adults only) and punch holes through leaves.

2. Encourage children to thread materials onto string to make a repeating pattern. Talk about the pattern with the children. Does it include different objects (conker, leaf, conker, leaf)? Or is it a shape, colour or size pattern. Twigs can be tied onto string, rather than threading, as can pine cones.

Ice numbers

What you need:

- Black marker pen
- White porous paper (kitchen towel is ideal)
- Clear plastic containers of various shapes and sizes
- A selection of small natural loose parts, pebbles, gravel, petals, small shells etc.
- Water
- Access to a freezer

What to do:

1. Draw a number onto a piece of paper with your marker pen. The number should soak through to the other side. (Be careful not to mark surfaces as you do this).

2. Turn over your paper to show a reversed version of the number.

3. Place your clear plastic container the right way up on top of the paper so you can see the reversed number through the bottom of the container.

4. Arrange your natural materials on the bottom of your container in the shape of the numeral.

5. Add water to cover the materials and carefully transfer to the freezer until frozen. In winter this activity can be done outdoors and left outside overnight to freeze ready for the morning if the temperature is cold enough.

6. Remove the ice block from the container, turn over and you will see the number the correct way round.

7. Add to water trays, sand trays or just leave out for children to explore.

Taking it forward

- Freeze sets of objects into ice so that children can count the objects and even match to their ice numbers.

- Place plastic number cookie cutter (those used for play dough) onto some play dough and push so the bottom is sealed. Add water and freeze to make frozen numbers, great for your water tray as they will float.

- Freeze large-scale numerals in larger containers such as dustbin lids or ice cream containers or even a paddling pool (this has to be done over night in freezing temperatures). Don't forget to reverse your numbers as you arrange them.

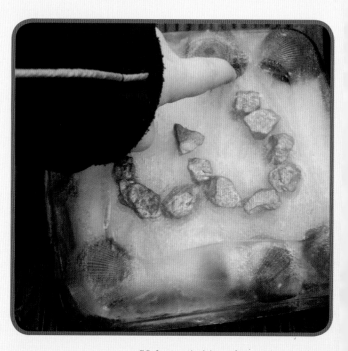

Top tip ⭐

Try placing a loop of string over the edge of your container before your freeze it or leave it out in the cold and you will be able to hang up your ice numbers in the morning.

What's in it for the children?

This is a lovely sensory way of exploring number recognition and simple counting whilst investigating the ice as it melts. A great example of maths and understanding the world integrated into one activity. Don't forget this is an activity for all seasons not just the colder weather!

Number splat!

What you need:

- A large white or clear plastic sheet
- A marker pen or laminated number cards
- Sponges or sponge balls (tie strips of sponge cloth together with cable ties to make these)
- A selection of watered-down paint or water coloured with chalk
- Pegs
- Large dice or a cube-shaped box painted to look like a dice

What to do:

1. Peg your sheet to a fence or wall.
2. If you use a white sheet then draw numbers on with your marker pens. If using a clear sheet then laminated numbers can be stuck to the reverse of the sheet so they can be splattered without getting soaked.
3. Roll the dice and encourage children to throw a sponge soaked in coloured water at the matching number on the sheet. Give children an extra go if they manage to hit the right number. If they miss then the next person has a turn.

Taking it forward

- Use pictures of groups of objects on the sheet so children have to match groups of objects with the numbers on the dice.

- Try using two dice and encouraging more able children to add the numbers together and then splat the sheet.

- Use a number dice rather than a spotty one to encourage numeral recognition.

What's in it for the children?

As well as lots of counting, number matching and recognition this activity is great for those children who learn best by 'doing' (kinesthetic learners) and encourages the development of muscles in arms, wrists and shoulders (essential for later pencil control as well as developing hand eye coordination).

> **Top tip** ⭐
>
> Clear decorating sheets from DIY stores are great for this activity.

Number pebbles

What you need:

- **A wide selection of river washed pebbles** (from garden centres - NOT from the beach or river!)
- **Acrylic paints**
- **Varnish**
- **Polished pebbles** (the kind used for house decoration)

What to do:

1. Paint your pebbles with numerals and varnish to make them fully water and weatherproof.

2. Make the number pebbles available for use as part of children's ongoing outdoor play. Encourage them to make number lines, talk about the numbers, and count objects to match the numerals.

Top tip

Using yacht varnish makes pebbles last longer. If you don't have acrylic paint then nail varnish works well for drawing numbers on small pebbles (keep away from children).

Taking it forward

- Make number lines with larger stones and encourage children to walk on or next to them (being mindful of safety at all times) counting as they step.

- Can you hide one of the number stones or turn it over and see if children can work out which number is missing?

- Try making number patterns with the pebbles and see if children can carry them on: 1,2,1,2 etc.

- Make collections of natural materials and find the number stone that matches.

- Make number stones with pictures of groups of objects e.g. 6 ladybirds or 4 flowers and see if you can match them up with the numerals.

What's in it for the children?

The tactile nature of number stones and pebbles allows children to explore numerals, ordering numbers and counting in a very unique sensory way.

Once you pop...

What you need:

- **A selection of crisp tubes** (the type with plastic lids)
- **A sharp knife**
- **Coloured paper or paint**
- **Sticky-back plastic**
- **Velcro**
- **Laminated numbers**
- **Pens**

What to do:

1. Cut the bottom off the crisp tube with a sharp knife (adult only).
2. Turn it upside down so the lid is now at the bottom.
3. Decorate the tube with paper and paint a different number on each one. When dry cover it with clear sticky-back plastic.
4. Put a Velcro square onto the tube.
5. Now place a strip of sticky Velcro onto a fence or pole.
6. Attach the tubes to the Velcro so they are at child height.
7. Encourage the children to find enough objects to match the numbers in the counting tubes. Position some baskets underneath so when they have finished they can take the lids off (the bottom!) and count the objects as they drop through the tubes into the baskets underneath.

Taking it forward

- Try changing the numbers on the tubes to shapes and collect shaped objects in the tubes.
- Put some objects into the tubes and encourage children to explore how many are in the tube and then find the correct number to match.

What's in it for the children?

This is a great activity for children who learn best by 'doing'. It provides an opportunity to explore counting objects as they drop them into the tubes, building on confidence to count moveable objects and to match and recognise numerals.

Top tip ⭐

Try not to leave out in heavy rain or you will end up with soggy tubes!

Planting with numbers

What you need:

- Strong glue
- Wooden or plastic plant marker sticks (from a garden centre)
- Plastic or foam numbers

What to do:

1. Glue the plastic numbers onto the plant sticks and allow to dry.

2. Encourage children to poke the sticks into the ground in order to make their own number lines.

3. Leave the number sticks out so children are able to use them as part of their ongoing play and exploration.

4. Try giving children some plastic plant sticks and dry wipe markers and encourage them to write and make their own number sticks and number lines.

Taking it forward

- Have a go at making a reverse number line and encourage children to count backwards as well as forwards.

- Place the sticks in front of terracotta pots and encourage children to sort natural objects into the pots to match the numeral.

- Hide one of the sticks and ask children to work out what number is missing?

- Ask children to find a stick which shows a specific number. Can they find one that is one more? One less? Etc.

What's in it for the children?

This is a lovely way of incorporating numbers and number lines into their everyday outdoor play. Children need lots of opportunities to count forwards and backwards in a variety of different situations.

Super sand swamp

What you need:

- Sand
- A builder's tray or similar
- Washing up liquid
- Warm water
- Powder paint (green is great!)
- Plastic dinosaurs

Taking it forward

- Compare the dinosaurs. Which is the biggest, longest, tallest, smallest etc.?

- Can you sort the dinosaurs according to size, type or colour?

- Hide laminated dinosaur number cards in the bottom of the tray and encourage children to move the swamp around to find them. This is all helps to build fine motor skills.

- Use purple powder paint instead of green and make an alien swamp. Count and sort aliens and space figures.

- Make some dinosaur footprints from foam or potatoes and use to make tracks in your swamp. How many can you see? Which ones are biggest? Can you find a smaller one?

What's in it for the children?

Using objects which really excite children will help to engage them in the activity and give you a good starting point for extending their learning further.

What to do:

1. Empty a bag of sand into your builder's tray.

2. Squirt a generous amount of washing up liquid onto the sand (about ¼ to ½ a bottle usually works).

3. Add water a little at a time and stir with hands until you get a frothy mousse-like texture. Add powder paint and mix to make a swamp.

4. Encourage children to take their dinosaurs on a number walk through the swamp, making the shape of the numeral in its trail. Try making a number with your dinosaur and see if the other children can tell what it is.

5. Encourage lots of talking about how many dinosaurs there are.

Collect and count

What you need:

- A selection of clear two litre plastic drink bottles
- Permanent marker pens or vinyl numbers (the type you put on your wheelie bins!)
- A wide selection of natural materials including pinecones, pebbles, shells, acorns, leaves, sticks, etc.

What to do:

1. Cut the tops off the bottles so you end up with clear containers.
2. Stick the numbers on the front of the containers or draw on with the marker pens.
3. Encourage children to fill the containers with the correct number of objects.

Taking it forward

- Use smaller clear drinks bottles to encourage children to sort and count smaller objects.
- Make number skittles with plastic bottles and rolling a ball to see what numbers they can knock over.

What's in it for the children?

Children need lots and lots of opportunities to count objects that they can move before they can count non-moveable objects. The more opportunities they get to sort and count different materials, the easier this skill gets. Working with natural materials allows children to do this in a way that makes links with outdoors.

Top tip ⭐

Sometimes putting a large pebble or some sand at the bottom of the container stops it falling over.

A number tree

What you need:

- Craft wire
- String
- Conkers
- Acorns
- Beads
- Weaving numbers
- Twigs

What to do:

1. Part of best practice in early years is to 'enable an engaging environment' for learning to take place in. For outdoor learning it is important to take the things which occur naturally in your setting and enhance them rather than try to add lots of artificial equipment.

2. Using the materials you have collected make an array of different numbers. Try threading beads onto numbers made from wire (or sticks tied together). Experiment with conkers or acorns threaded onto wire numbers. Try glass beads stuck onto CD's in the shape of numbers.

3. Hang all of your numbers from a tree or bush to offer lots of opportunities to explore them in different lights and differing weather. Try adding ribbons to see them blow in the wind.

4. Add pre-bought weaving numbers (available from TTS) threaded with beads and ribbons and your number tree will become a favourite with children of all ages!

Taking it forward

- Make more numbers and display them throughout your outdoor area. Organise a number hunt: how many 3's can you find? Can you find the number which comes next etc.?

What's in it for the children?

A great chance for children to explore numbers and name them in the outdoor environment, this activity enhances the learning environment rather than imposing fabricated plastic numbers onto a natural environment. As the numbers move in the wind or glint in the sun children will be encouraged to explore and talk about light and the seasons from first hand experience.

Top tip ⭐

If you don't have a tree or bush in your outdoor area, try planting one in an old tyre or just sinking a large branch from an old tree into the ground to give you something to hang all sorts of things on (make sure it is secure at all times).

Splish, splash!

What you need:

- **Suitable outdoor clothing**
- **Puddles** (even in summer you can have fun splashing in puddles. If there's no rain, then make your own!)
- **Pavement chalks**

What to do:

1. Find a puddle. Have some fun jumping in it first!

2. Then draw a line around the outside of the puddle with your chalk.

3. Leave the puddle for an hour or so and then come back and draw around it again.

4. Did your puddle get bigger or smaller? Why do you think it did that?

5. Leave it a bit longer and measure again.

Taking it forward

- Try mixing powder paint in a few puddles (or crushed up chalk) and leave them to dry. You will be left with a coloured puddle shapes on the pavement. Which is the biggest? Smallest?

- Draw around a puddle. Now see if you can find a way of making it bigger or think of a way to make it smaller?

What's in it for the children?

Children need to have a chance to do lots of comparisons of size in lots of different real life situations. This activity helps to build on their understanding of size and concepts of big, bigger, small, and smaller whilst providing lots of opportunities for early science problem solving and discussion.

Top tip ⭐

Put coloured chalk into a zip food bag and hit it with a hammer to make chalk dust for using in puddles.

Measure the raindrops

What you need:

- Clear plastic two litre plastic drink bottle
- Scissors
- Permanent marker pen
- Ruler

Taking it forward

- Use a ruler to mark 1cm intervals up the side of the bottle. Encourage children to talk about which number the water is nearest to and explain that you are 'measuring'.

- Try putting a few drops of food colouring into the bottom of the bottle so that the rainwater appears coloured as it collects for extra sensory interest.

- Keep a record over a week of how much it rains. Talk about more, less, most, least and the days of the week.

What's in it for the children?

Children need to experience measuring in real situations so that they begin to understand why we need to measure some things and that maths is used for a reason. This activity allows children to explore weather whilst building on their mathematical measuring language.

Top tip

Always pour water away after a couple of days to avoid it going stagnant.

What to do:

1. Cut around the top of the bottle and then turn the top upside down and place back into the bottle to act as a funnel (see below).

2. Leave the bottle somewhere in the open to collect rainwater.

3. Mark where the water comes up to with a pen, leave and then mark again the next day.

4. Encourage talk using words like more, less, empty, full, etc.

I spy... how many?

What you need:

- **Laminated sheets with picture clues** on e.g. 3 leaves, 2 pebbles etc. (scavenger list)
- **Dry wipe marker pens**
- **Some baskets for collecting** (the ones you get in charity shops for flower arranging are ideal)

What to do:

1. Give children their scavenger list.
2. Encourage them to talk about what's on the list i.e. 3 leaves, 2 pebbles etc.
3. Let them have fun collecting the objects on their list and tick or crossing things off as they find them.

Taking it forward

- A sheet with just the objects and a blank for the number so children are able to fill in how many they find.
- Try scavenger hunts for colours, shapes and sizes too. Try finding things that are bigger than... or longer than...

What's in it for the children?

This really encourages children to look closely at their outdoor environment as well as counting as they go. Again, lots of opportunities to count objects that move as well as observing shapes, size and colour in the natural world.

Collection pockets

- **Pockets** (clear plastic food bags with zip tops) **or clear plastic zip wallets**
- Dry wipe marker pens
- Laminated number cards

What to do:

1. Attach the 'pockets' at a low, child height. Stapling them to a wooden fence, a shed or piece of wooden trellis is ideal.
2. Draw on numbers or add number cards to the pockets.
3. Encourage children to explore their outdoor surroundings and find enough objects to put onto the pockets to match the numerals.

Taking it forward

- Mix up the numbers so they are not in order (this encourages numeral recognition as opposed to rote counting).
- Add a number and a colour card to encourage children to find say '3 red things' or '5 green things'. Extend this to shapes e.g. 4 square things etc.
- Give children blank laminated cards and dry wipe pens and encourage them to make their own cards for sorting and counting.
- Have a go at adding objects to the pockets and giving children the number cards to put in the correct pockets.

What's in it for the children?

Children are able to explore lots of sorting, counting and matching using these resources. A lovely, unimposing addition to an outdoor environment which encourages children to explore their outdoor surroundings and work together as well as on their own.

Shape bubbles

What you need:

- Wire cutters
- Wire coat hangers
- Electrical tape
- Bubble mixture
- A large bucket

What to do:

1. Cut the hook off your coat hanger (adults only).
2. Bend the hanger wire to make a large shaped bubble blower.
3. Use electrical tape if needed to cover any sharp wire ends.
4. Fill the bucket with bubble mixture.
5. Dip your large shaped bubble wands into the bucket and see if you can make a long shaped bubble. Which shape makes the best bubbles? Encourage children to use the correct shape names as they explore with their bubble blowers.

Taking it forward

- Make a selection of different shaped bubble blowers.
- Make smaller shaped bubble blowers.

What's in it for the children?

A really fun and physical way of recognising and exploring with shapes at the same time as lots of early science exploration of bubbles and the way they behave.

Top tip ⭐

Running with the bubble wand will help to produce really big long bubbles (staying safe as you run!)

Shadow numbers

What you need:

- Pegs
- Some garden netting or a net curtain
- A set of foam floor numbers (the kind that fit together to make a mat)

What to do:

1. Peg up the netting to form a canopy in a sunny part of your outdoor area. You can create a den underneath with cushions to make it inviting for children to crawl in and explore.
2. Rest a selection of the numbers and their silhouettes across the netting (peg in place if needs be).
3. When the sun shines observe the numbers that the shade produces across the ground.
4. If you cannot get hold of foam numbers then why not try and make some card templates and use these instead.

Taking it forward

- Create your own number mobile by attaching some of the numbers onto twigs and hanging them somewhere sunny so children can watch the shadows move as the mobile sways in the breeze.

What's in it for the children?

Children need to experience numeral recognition in every situation possible. This activity allows them to explore numbers as well as prompting discussion about the weather and light and shadows.

Top tip ⭐

Select your spot carefully and you should be able to get a shadow all year long, even the coldest of winter days can be sunny!

Shadow play

What you need:

- A selection of sticks of different lengths
- Some acrylic paints and brushes
- Some pavement chalks
- Sunshine!

What to do:

1. Choose some sticks and decorate them with the paints and allow to dry. (This doesn't affect their shadow making ability but helps to make the sticks more appealing.)

2. When dry, stick them into the ground so that they cast a shadow.

3. Encourage children to draw along the shadows with chalk and talk about the different lengths.

4. Leave the sticks for an hour or so (doing this around midday and early afternoon will be more dramatic).

5. Return to the sticks and draw along the shadows now with a different coloured chalk. Children will notice that not only has the shadow moved but it will have shortened or lengthened dependent on whether you are heading towards or away from the point when the sun is directly over head (in the UK this is usually about 1-2 pm) and will produce the shortest shadows if any at all.

Taking it forward

- Try drawing around the shadows of other objects over time and see what happens.
- Try drawing around your own shadows over time.

What's in it for the children?

This is a great way of children exploring lots of early science with light and shadows in a uniquely outdoor environment whilst having first hand experience and exploration of length and the language of measuring.

Shape ahoy!

What to do:

1. Establish an area for running around safely. Place the shapes around the area and talk about what shape they are as you put them out.

2. Ask the children to run around in between the shapes as if they were pirates sailing the seas.

3. When you shout 'wind blows harder' they have to run faster. If you call 'there's a storm brewing' they can run around turning as they do. When you shout 'shipwreck... square' all the children try and run to the square shape.

4. If anyone falls into the sea (puts two feet off the shape they are out).

5. Try again this time shouting 'shipwreck and another shape'.

6. Keep going until only a few children remain. Then start to take away some of the shapes. The winner is the last person on the last shape.

Taking it forward

- Put the shapes out like a mini 'Twister' type game. Call out instructions like 'a hand on a square' or 'a foot on a circle'.

- Hold up objects you have found in the outdoor area e.g. a hoop or a brick and see if children can run to the shape that matches the object you have in your hand.

What's in it for the children?

This is a good way of engaging children who like to learn by moving around (kinesthetic learners) as they build their knowledge of shapes. It is also great for communication and language skills as it encourages listening and following simple instructions in a fun and very physical way.

Top tip ⭐

Make sure your shapes are on a non-slip surface to avoid injury.

48

Sprinklers of all sizes

What you need:

- **Clear plastic containers of all sizes** (plastic drinks bottles are ideal – two and three litre bottles in different shapes)
- **Scissors**
- **Screwdriver or bradle**
- **String or wire**
- **A water tray**

What to do:

1. Cut the tops off the bottles, ensuring there are no sharp edges.

2. Make small holes in the bottoms using a screwdriver or bradle (adult task) so that water can flow freely through. You could make different numbers or sizes of holes to increase or decrease the flow of water in differing containers.

3. Either use the clear water sprinklers freely in water play or suspend them in a line to hang over the water tray.

4. Encourage children to explore filling them with water and observing it sprinkling out. Which needs the most water? Which is biggest, smallest etc.? When is the sprinkler full? Empty? Etc.

Taking it forward

- Put holes in the bottom of big buckets and use in sand play. Children are able to really feel the concept of 'heavy' first hand.

- Try providing different coloured sands and watching as it flows through to mix and make patterns.

- Can children order the sprinklers according to size?

- Can they count how many smaller scoops or cups it takes to fill one of the sprinklers?

What's in it for the children?

The joy of outdoor learning is that children can gain access to equipment on a scale not available to indoor play. This activity allows children to explore large containers and gain a first hand insight into heavy weights and large sizes whilst exploring the vocabulary of capacity (full, empty etc.) and size.

Web slinging number fun

What you need:

- **Spaghetti** (cooked and cooled)
- **Paint in a variety of colours**
- **Large sheets of paper**
- **Masking tape**
- **Laminated super hero figures**
- **Small plastic drinks bottles**
- **Dry wipe marker pens**

What to do:

1. Colour the spaghetti with the paint leaving it quite wet.
2. Cover a large area of your outdoor area with paper (taping several sheets together to make one big canvas).
3. Write large numbers on the paper up to 10.
4. Encourage children to be Spider-Man and to fling their webs (spaghetti) at a specific number (bottle).

Taking it forward

- Try using a large dice. Throw your web spaghetti at the correct number to match the dice.
- Throw two dice, add them together and throw webs at the answer.

What's in it for the children?

This multi-sensory activity is great for building muscles in arms, shoulders and the back which will be essential in later pencil control as well as being a really physical maths activity ideal for those learners who prefer to be 'doing'. It can be left out in later days and weeks for children to use as part of their on-going play.

Going potty

What you need:

- A selection of terracotta pots in a wide variety of sizes (very small ones can be purchased from craft shops in the floristry dept)
- A wide selection of natural materials for sorting and counting, including conkers, pebbles, gravel, petals, leaves, seeds, acorns etc.
- Coloured chalk

What to do:

1. Chalk numbers on to the front of your pots and ask children to count natural materials into them to match the numeral.

2. Children can be encouraged to problem solve if you write larger amounts on smaller pots, encouraging them to find smaller objects and to use size words such as too big, smaller, etc.

Taking it forward

- Order the pots in size order. Can you stack them inside each other? (a kind of pot version of Russian dolls!)
- Try putting the same number on lots of different pots to focus on a particular number.

What's in it for the children?

Children need lots of opportunities to count moveable objects if they are to gain an understanding of what a particular number means (understanding the 'oneness of one'). This activity also has lots of scope for including the resources in open-ended child led learning if made available on a daily basis.

Tallying up!

What you need:

- Camouflage netting
- Spotter cards with a selection of outdoor objects e.g. tree, bird, leaf (printed and laminated)
- Clipboards
- Dry wipe marker pens
- Binoculars

Top tip

If it's birds you are spotting, try building your hide close to an area where you have placed birdseed or near a Buddleia bush if your looking out for butterflies.

Taking it forward

- Try spotting things which are all the same colour e.g. tree, grass, leaf, ball etc.
- Look for things that move (aeroplane, bird, car etc.)
- Use a magnifying glass and go spotting and tallying for small objects or mini beasts.

What's in it for the children?

This activity helps children to build on their understanding of one object for each mark on the tally chart and hence a better understanding of what numbers stand for. This activity is great for actively encouraging children to work together to find things and to record what they see.

What to do:

1. Use the netting to create a little hide somewhere in a corner of your outdoor area big enough to accommodate a few children.

2. Encourage children to use their binoculars to spot the things on the spotter list. Demonstrate how they can mark a tally on the spotter card each time they see a particular thing.

3. Work together to count up how many of each thing the children were able to spot. (Taking a quick scan of the sheet will give you a permanent record for future discussion).

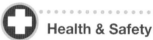

Health & Safety

Always show children how to use binoculars safely and NOT to point them directly at the sun.

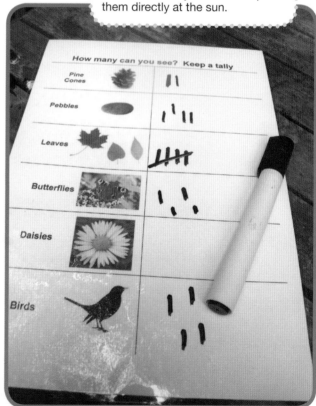

Big stick, little stick

What you need:

- A selection of sticks of different lengths and widths
- Acrylic paints and brushes

Taking it forward

- Measure using your stick e.g. a door is … sticks long. A bench is … sticks wide.

- Paint a long stick in equal coloured sections (say red, blue, red, blue etc.). Use your stick to measure objects e.g. a bat is 3 and a bit long, a ball is 2 wide etc.

- Take a collection of unpainted sticks and see if you can sort according to length either laid out on the ground or vertically stuck into the grass or mud.

- Try making holes through a set of sticks of different lengths and string them up in order to make a stick mobile with biggest at the bottom and smallest at the top etc.

What's in it for the children?

Long before children can use a ruler to measure they need a chance to use other objects to make size and length comparisons (non-standard measures). Using sticks is a great and fun way of using natural resources to explore length and early measuring skills as well as developing language skills. Painting the sticks just makes an open-ended resource even more special than it was!

What to do:

1. Select a stick each.

2. Explore painting patterns on your stick and leave to dry (don't forget to talk about the patterns and colours as you create!).

3. Use your sticks to explore measuring the length of objects around your outdoor setting. Can the children find something longer, shorter, the same length? Can they make collections of things which are the same length or order them according to length e.g. smallest at one side and longest at the other? Try with someone else's stick. Do they get the same set of objects?

Top tip ★

Explore stick measure as part of exploring stories such as **Stick man** by Julia Donaldson, **Stanley's Stick** by Neal Layton or **Not a stick** by Antoinette Portis.

Mushroom maths

What you need:

- Wooden door/drawer knobs in various sizes
- Red and white acrylic paint
- Wood varnish

What to do:

1. Paint various numbers of spots onto the top of the doorknobs to look like toadstools. Varnish to preserve and allow for outdoor use.

2. Encourage children to order the toadstools according to the number of spots. (Don't forget to make at least one toadstool with zero spots on it).

3. Encourage children to sort the toadstools according to size either into sets or in a line with smallest at one end and biggest at the other.

4. Play matching pairs with the toadstools, can you find two toadstools with the same number of spots?

5. Take two toadstools and ask children to work out how many spots altogether?

6. Can they find a toadstool with one more or one less spots?

Taking it forward

- Paint the tops of tree stumps to look like toadstool tops with different numbers of spots. Use for matching and counting talk.

- Try extending your toadstools collection by making more toadstools with different coloured tops and with larger numbers on. Encourage children to sort according to colour and numbers.

What's in it for the children?

A lovely outdoor themed activity which encourages children to explore counting, sorting and matching with a unique resource which is both cheap to make and easy to extend. Great as an extension to a fairy garden small world play experience.

Top tip ⭐

Painting the numeral on the bottom which matches the number of spots on the top of the toadstools acts a great self-checking system.

I spy treasure!

What you need:

- A sand tray
- A selection of play gold coins, gold gravel pieces (available from garden centres or you can spray paint your own) **and some silver shells** (spray paint a selection of shells with silver paint)
- A large gravel sieve

What to do:

1. Bury some of the 'treasure' in the sand.

2. Children can use the sieve to find the treasure. Each time encourage them to talk about how many pieces they have found.

3. Try collecting your treasure in a bag. You can count out and sort your treasure afterwards.

Top tip ⭐

Never spray paint objects indoors - always do in a well-ventilated area (adult activity).

Taking it forward

- Bury the gold coins after you have written numbers on them in marker pen. What numbers are the children digging up? Can they count out the same number of gold pieces? Can they put their gold coins in order according to the numbers?

- Use coins with both numbers and spots on. Can children match a coin with spots to the correct coin with a number on?

- Bury the silver shells. Can children order their shells according to size? Can they match two the same shape or size? How many shells can they find?

What's in it for the children?

Key to children's exploration of numbers and early maths is for it to be an engaging part of their integrated play experience. This idea offers lots of scope for sorting, matching, counting and patterning as part of on-going sand play. The use of treasure objects makes it a real 'invitation to play'.

Witch's cookery class

What you need:

- *The Witch's Kitchen* by Nick Sharratt

- A wide selection of metal bowls, plates, cups saucepans and kitchen utensils

- Milk crates or wooden vegetable crates

- Some mud!

- Herbs, petals, grass, conkers, pinecones, glitter, water, pebbles, shells etc.

- Wooden spoons (the bigger the better)

- Water

- Some witches' hats

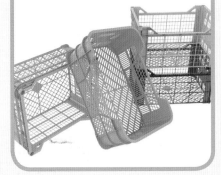

What to do:

1. Read *The Witch's Kitchen* by Nick Sharratt with the children and build yourself an outdoor witch's mud kitchen using the equipment above.

2. Make a witch's recipe card showing what to add for certain spells. Make your recipes simple and easy to follow e.g. 2 gold stones, 3 daisies, 2 scoops of chocolate mud and a cup of pond water etc.

3. Work with the children to count and find the correct ingredients and to mix them up in their kitchen. Encourage lots of talk about more, less, empty, full etc. as well as counting and matching.

Top tip ⭐

Use metal plates, spoons, etc. wherever possible to keep the equipment uniquely 'outdoors' and to help make it last longer.

Taking it forward

- Leave children to explore their witch's kitchen and follow the recipes or to write/develop their own witch's brew.

- Try putting out a paddling pool and letting children mix their mixture in it with a very long wide spoon or a stick.

What's in it for the children?

Recipes are always great for helping children to develop their counting and measuring skills. This activity takes a traditional baking activity and makes it outdoor and original. Ideal for those children who prefer to be outdoors and up to their necks in mud! It is also great for developing co-operative play and language and communication skills as children work together on this large outdoor scale to create their own potions and mixtures.

Nature trip strips

What you need:

- Strips of card
- Strips of double-sided sticky tape
- Sellotape, paper clips or a stapler

What to do:

1. Place a piece of double-sided tape onto a strip of card keeping the second side still covered with the paper seal. Pin, staple or clip the strip of card to form either a wristband or a crown like headband. Ensure all interested children have one each.

2. As a group go on a hunt around your outdoor area.

3. Take off the remaining tape paper so that your wristband or crown is now sticky.

4. What colours can you find? Each time you find an object stick it to your crown or band. Build up your collection of objects according to colour, shape, size etc.

Taking it forward

- Have a selection of bands and crowns made up and leave out with a wide selection of natural materials. Encourage children to use the materials to make patterns on their crowns or bands.

- See how many green things the children can find and stick on their bands.

- Use strips of card and sticky tape laid flat so children can just stick on patterns and groups of objects, encourage them to talk about their choices and to look at size, colour and shape as well as counting.

What's in it for the children?

In early maths, children need to recognise similarities and differences and to be able to sort a wide variety of objects according to different criteria. This activity helps children build on their colour sorting skills using natural resources and as they collect the pieces on their bands they also get the chance to begin making simple patterns according to shape or size etc.

Top tip

Leave the second paper seal on until you get to where you are going to look for objects, it ensures maximum stickiness is retained!

Twig number trails

What you need:

- A selection of twigs and sticks
- Number list

Taking it forward

- Encourage the children to lay their own number trails, making the number shapes from all sorts of natural materials including twigs, shells, conkers, bark etc. This all helps to build number recognition and formation skills.

- Use wire (use craft or florist wire – it's easy to manipulate) or string to tie some sticks together to make rigid numerals which you can either let children move around and order into a natural number line or sort objects to match them.

What's in it for the children?

As well as a great chance to recognise numerals in a natural environment and give children lots of opportunities for matching and counting, this activity also helps to develop co -operative working skills and can aid in developing language and communication skills.

Top tip ⭐

Laminate your number list and give children a dry wipe pen for going on their number hunt.

What to do:

1. Use the sticks to make numerals and arrows so that children can follow a number trail. This can be done in a different ways:

   - Get children to follow the number trail in order starting at 0 or 1 and counting forwards.

   - Give the children a list of numbers, say 0-9 on a sheet of paper, and a pencil and ask them to hunt for the different numbers and tick them off when they have found them.

   - Make lots of the same number (say number 4) around the outdoor setting and see how many of them the children can find. Use lots of different sized numbers from very tiny ones to huge ones made from logs, this will encourage use if size language as well as numbers.

Right on target

What you need:

- Laminated number pictures of characters appealing to your cohort of children (princesses, superheroes, Peppa pig etc.). Use old comics, birthday cards, and wrapping paper or find images on the Internet.

- Pins, stapler or sticky tak

- Water pistols

- Bucket of water

What to do:

1. Fix your number cards to a wall or fence at and above child level.

2. Encourage children to fill the water pistols and shoot at specific targets e.g. 'Can you shoot number 3?' 'Which one is number 5?' Etc.

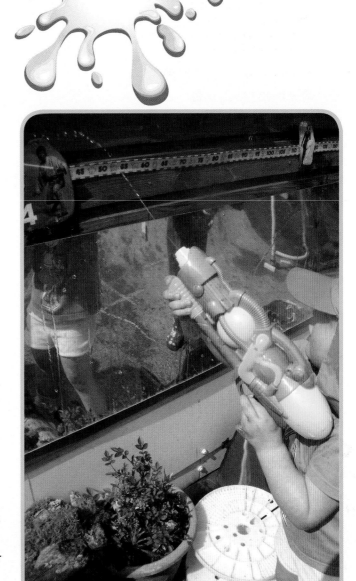

Taking it forward

- In groups have a race to see who can be the first to shoot a number when shouted out.

- See if the children can shoot the cards in order.

- See if the children can shoot the number and then 'one more' or 'one less'.

- Draw a numeral onto a blackboard or concrete surface and see if children can squirt over the top of the numeral with their water pistols.

- Make laminated numbers and stand them up on a table, log or outdoors and see if children can knock over certain numbers using their water pistols.

What's in it for the children?

Children need lots of opportunities to recognise numerals in lots of situations and some children learn better by 'doing'. This activity is particularly good for these kinds of learners and is great for engaging boys as well as girls. Also, squeezing and pumping water pistols is great for building muscles in hands, wrists and arms essential for pre writing development.

Sharp shooter

What you need:

- Chalk
- Large pump action water pistols

What to do:

1. On walls and fences draw a selection of very big and smaller numbers.

2. Encourage children to stand at a distance and try to squirt the water pistol around the shape of the numeral.

3. Encourage lots of talk about what the number is and how you can create it with your water pistol.

4. Try asking children to find the number that is one more or one less than another number and to squirt that, or even to add two numbers together and squirt the answer.

Taking it forward

- Make the difference in sizes of the numbers greater to encourage bigger and smaller movements to cover the numbers with water.

- Try standing further and further away from the numbers.

- In winter, fill the water pistols with coloured warm water and shoot onto snow or frosty surfaces.

What's in it for the children?

This activity is a great combination of motor skills development, helping to build those all important muscles needed eventually for writing, at the same time as developing number recognition and numeral formation.